DISCOVER AMERICA

ALASKA

Leslie Strudwick

MEDIA ENHANCED BOOKS
AV2 BY WEIGL
ADDED VALUE • AUDIO VISUAL

www.av2books.com

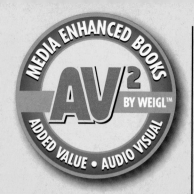

AV² provides enriched content that supplements and complements this book. Weigl's AV² books strive to create inspired learning and engage young minds in a total learning experience.

Your AV² Media Enhanced books come alive with...

Audio
Listen to sections of the book read aloud.

Key Words
Study vocabulary, and complete a matching word activity.

Video
Watch informative video clips.

Quizzes
Test your knowledge.

Embedded Weblinks
Gain additional information for research.

Slide Show
View images and captions, and prepare a presentation.

Try This!
Complete activities and hands-on experiments.

... and much, much more!

Go to **www.av2books.com**, and enter this book's unique code.

BOOK CODE

R 2 6 4 5 5 5

AV² by Weigl brings you media enhanced books that support active learning.

Published by AV² by Weigl
350 5th Avenue, 59th Floor
New York, NY 10118
Website: www.av2books.com

Library of Congress Cataloging-in-Publication Data
Names: Strudwick, Leslie, 1970- author.
Title: Alaska : the last frontier / Leslie Strudwick.
Other titles: Alaska.
Description: New York, NY : AV2 by Weigl, [2016] | Series: Discover America | Includes index.
Identifiers: LCCN 2015044631 (print) | LCCN 2015044980 (ebook) | ISBN 9781489648181 (hard cover : alk. paper) | ISBN 9781489648198 (soft cover : alk. paper) | ISBN 9781489648204 (Multi-User eBook)
Subjects: LCSH: Alaska--Juvenile literature.
Classification: LCC F904.3 .S793 2016 (print) | LCC F904.3 (ebook) | DDC 979.8--dc23
LC record available at http://lccn.loc.gov/2015044631

Printed in the United States of America, in Brainerd, Minnesota
1 2 3 4 5 6 7 8 9 20 19 18 17 16

042016
040816

Project Coordinator Heather Kissock
Art Director Terry Paulhus

Photo Credits
Every reasonable effort has been made to trace ownership and to obtain permission to reprint copyright material. The publisher would be pleased to have any errors or omissions brought to their attention so that they may be corrected in subsequent printings. The publisher acknowledges Getty Images, Corbis Images, iStock, Wikimedia, Shutterstock, and Alamy as its primary image suppliers for this title.

ALASKA

Contents

AV² Code.................................... 2
Discover Alaska............................ 4

THE LAND
Beginnings 6
Where is Alaska? 8
Land Features 10
Climate 12
Nature's Resources 14
Vegetation 16
Wildlife.................................. 18

ECONOMY
Tourism 20
Primary Industries....................... 22
Goods and Services 24

HISTORY
Native Americans......................... 26
Exploring the Land 28
The First Settlers....................... 30
History Makers........................... 32

CULTURE
The People Today 34
State Government 36
Celebrating Culture 38
Arts and Entertainment 40
Sports and Recreation 42

Get to Know Alaska....................... 44
Brain Teasers............................ 46
Key Words/Index 47
Log on to www.av2books.com 48

STATE FLOWER
Forget-Me-Not

STATE BIRD
Willow Ptarmigan

STATE TREE
Sitka Spruce

STATE FLAG
Alaska

STATE MAMMAL
Moose

STATE SEAL
Alaska

Nickname
The Last Frontier

Motto
North to the Future

Song
"Alaska's Flag," words by
Marie Drake and music
by Elinor Dusenbury

Population
(2010 Census) 710,231
Ranked 47th state

Entered the Union
January 3, 1959, as the 49th state

Capital
Juneau

Discover Alaska

Alaska is the northernmost state in the United States. Almost one-third of its land is within the Arctic Circle. The state is so far north that in certain areas during the summer the sun never sets. In the winter, however, daylight is very limited.

Extending to the southeast from the Alaska peninsula is a strip of land called the Panhandle. This part of Alaska borders the Canadian province of British Columbia. Most of the Panhandle's land is covered by the Tongass National Forest, the United States' largest national forest.

Alaska's scenic beauty offers wonderful outdoor opportunities for residents and tourists alike. Among the popular pastimes are hiking in the mountains, sailing past **glaciers**, and enjoying the dazzling northern lights. Alaska also attracts adventure seekers who glide over the icy **tundra** in dogsleds.

Alaska's landscape contains many mountains and includes 17 of North America's 20 tallest peaks. Denali, at 20,320 feet, is North America's tallest peak, attracting expert mountain climbers to scale its snowfield-covered rock.

The Land

There are more than **3,000 rivers** in Alaska and more than **3 million lakes**. The largest is Lake Iliama, with an area of **1,000 square miles**.

The area of Alaska is so grand that the state of **Rhode Island** could fit inside it **425 times**.

The Alaskan Railroad is owned by the state of Alaska. The route spans more than 500 miles.

The Klondike gold rush saw nearly 100,000 people migrating to Alaska to find their fortune.

Beginnings

T he name *Alaska* means "mainland" or "great land" in the language of the Aleuts, an Alaska Native group. The area of Alaska makes up almost one-fifth of the total area of the United States. Both geography and climate have made it difficult to develop and explore Alaska. It is indeed, as the state's nickname says, the United States' last frontier.

Russians established the first European settlement in 1784 at Three Saints Bay, near what is now Kodiak. Fur trapping became their primary trade. The native Aleut population was affected by these European settlers. Many died from diseases brought by the Russians, and others were overworked in the hunting of fur seals.

Alaska has played an important part in the history of the nation. The land was purchased from Russia in 1867, nearly a century before it became the 49th state in 1959. Miners from the lower 48 U.S. states traveled to Alaska in search of gold in the late 1800s. Many of these settlers fell in love with the wilderness and chose to stay. These new settlers lived among the Alaska Natives, who had inhabited the region for thousands of years.

Where is ALASKA?

Alaska is bordered by the Arctic Ocean and the Beaufort Sea to the north. On the east, it shares a border with the Yukon Territory and British Columbia, both part of Canada. To the south, the Gulf of Alaska and the Pacific Ocean form its border. The Bering Strait and the Bering Sea lie to its west. Alaska's Little Diomede Island, in the Bering Strait, is only 2.5 miles from the border of Russia.

RUSSIA

United States Map

Alaska   Hawai'i

MAP LEGEND

- ⬛ Alaska
- ☆ Capital City
- ● Major City
- Denali National Park
- Glacier Bay National Park
- ⬜ Canada, Russia
- ⬜ Water

SCALE   0 — 250 miles

1 Juneau

Juneau has been the capital of Alaska since 1906. Located in southeastern Alaska on the Gastineau Channel, Juneau has a population of about 31,000. In 1970, Juneau merged with the city of Douglas, located on an island across the channel. It is now 3,248 square miles in area, the largest city in area in the United States.

2 Denali National Park

Denali National Park was established on February 26, 1917. The park encompasses 6 million acres of untouched Alaskan wilderness. The town of Kantishna sits at the center of the park. It features 135 residents during the summer and no one lives there during the winter.

ALASKA

CANADA

4

2

Fairbanks

Juneau

3

1

Pacific Ocean

3 **Glacier Bay National Park**

With 3.3 million acres of rugged terrain, Glacier Bay National Park is also a World Heritage Site. This internationally protected area features many **ecosystems**, from glaciers to coastline. The park has created a safe space for plants and animals in and out of the water.

4 **Fairbanks**

Born from the Gold Rush era of the early 1900s, Fairbanks is still capitalizing on the minerals that can be found in the nearby mountains. In the winter, Fairbanks receives a little more than three hours of sunlight and is a great location to spot the northern lights.

Land Features

Alaska is by far the biggest state in the United States with a land area of 571,951 square miles. It measures 1,420 miles from north to south and 2,400 miles from east to west. The land varies from flat, bush-covered areas to mountain ranges.

Alaska's land has many outstanding features. It has the largest number of glaciers in the United States and more than 130 active volcanoes. The largest national parks in the United States are found in Alaska.

Wrangell–St. Elias National Park

Wrangell–St. Elias National Park is the country's largest national park. It measures more than 20,000 square miles. Nine states are smaller than the park.

Alaska's Coastline

Alaska's coastline extends for more than 6,600 miles. Including islands, the state has nearly 34,000 miles of shoreline.

Tracy Arm Fjord

In the winter, 20 percent of the Fjord is completely covered in ice. In the summer, visitors can see floating ice in sizes ranging from the size of a human hand to the length of a 3-story building.

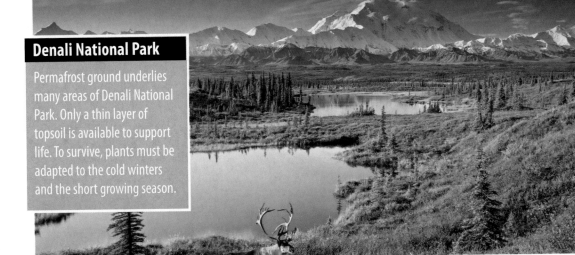

Denali National Park

Permafrost ground underlies many areas of Denali National Park. Only a thin layer of topsoil is available to support life. To survive, plants must be adapted to the cold winters and the short growing season.

Climate

The beauty of the Alaskan landscape makes up for the sometimes harsh climate. The temperatures in the south are quite mild in summer. The west, which borders the ocean, receives more rain and snow and is often cooler than the rest of the state. In the north, temperatures can hover near the freezing point in July. However, the majority of people living in and visiting Alaska are in the south and central regions of the state. They may experience temperatures of –40° Fahrenheit in the winter, but they enjoy an average summer temperature of about 55°F.

Average Annual Precipitation Across Alaska

There can be huge differences in the amount of precipitation that different parts of Alaska typically receive. What do you think causes these differences?

LEGEND

Average Annual Precipitation (in inches) 1971-2000

<4	43–47
4–8	47–51
8–12	51–55
12–16	55–59
16–20	59–79
20–24	79–98
24–27	98–118
27–31	118–157
31–35	157–197
35–39	197–295
39–43	>295

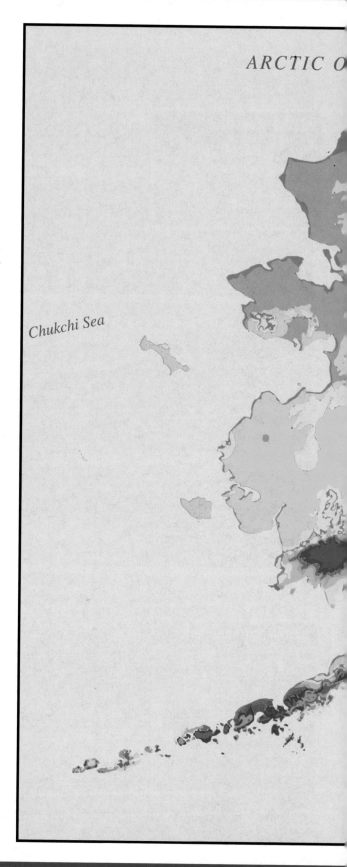

ARCTIC O

Chukchi Sea

N

Scale 0 ▬▬▬▬ 5 Miles

AN

CANADA

Gulf of Alaska

PACIFIC OCEAN

Nature's Resources

Alaska is rich in natural resources. There are fish in the water, trees covering the land, and minerals in the ground. Gold was the first natural resource that brought prosperity and settlers to Alaska. Large amounts of gold were discovered beginning in the 1870s, drawing thousands of **prospectors** to the area in search of the precious metal. Gold mining still exists today, but it does not employ as many workers as before. There are also mines for coal, silver, and zinc.

Alaska's two main foreign **exports** are precious metals and fish. In fact, the state is the nation's top exporter of fish. Leading catches include salmon, halibut, and shellfish such as crab. Fishing contributes nearly $2 billion to the state's economy each year.

Commercial herring fishing made more than $30 million for the state of Alaska in 2012.

Oil and natural gas are the state's most important natural resources. More than 80 percent of the taxes collected by the state come from the oil and gas industry. Most of Alaska's known oil deposits are in the far north. The Trans-Alaska Pipeline, which extends north–south for 800 miles, transports most of the oil produced in the state to Valdez, in southern Alaska.

Oil fields in Prudhoe Bay are mined for crude oil. This unrefined oil is then shipped to refineries in Valdez for processing.

Gold mining is not just part of Alaska's past. Recreational gold mining has become part of Alaska's tourism economy.

Vegetation

From forest to marsh, Alaska has a variety of plant life. Among Alaska's plant life are bushes that produce juicy berries, including the lowbush cranberry, strawberries, blueberries, and cloudberries. Pine forests are found in many of Alaska's highlands and along the coast. Other trees that are common in Alaska are spruce, cottonwood, Alaska birch, and larch. Tongass National Forest and Chugach National Forest are the largest national forests in the United States.

Alaska's small human population and untouched wilderness areas keep the state's environment pure and healthy. Plants that have been in Alaska for thousands of years continue to exist. However, as more people have sought to make use of the many resources found in the state, some of these plants have become **threatened**.

Monkshood

Monkshood is beautiful to look at, but all parts of the plant are poisonous if ingested.

Boreal Forest

Boreal forests are found in Alaska's interior. They are the product of extreme temperatures and slow, short growing periods.

Birch Trees

Three varieties of birch trees grow in Alaska. One kind, Kenai canoe birch, has been used by Alaska Natives to make canoes.

Lingonberry, or Lowbush Cranberry

The lingonberry, or lowbush cranberry, is the most common berry growing in Alaska.

Wildlife

Alaska is home to a wide variety of animals in the sky, on land, and in water. There are about 400 different bird species in Alaska. The eagle is the largest bird found in the state. Other common birds include owls, hawks, and falcons. The Arctic tern, found in Alaska during the summer, spends the winter in Antarctica, some 10,000 miles away.

Bears are common in Alaska. Brown bears (also known as grizzly bears), black bears, and polar bears all make their home in the state. Also found in Alaska are beavers, reindeer, wolverines, wolves, deer, elks, bison, foxes, moose, mountain sheep, mountain goats, and lynx.

Alaska's waters are home to many fish and marine mammals. More than a dozen different species of whales can be seen off Alaska's coast. They include the bowhead whale, the humpback whale, the killer whale, and the narwhal. Other sea animals include otters, walruses, and seals.

Sockeye Salmon
Every spring, millions of salmon return to Alaska to **spawn**. Adult salmon may swim as far as 2,000 miles.

American Bald Eagle

The bald eagle was officially adopted as the U.S. national emblem on June 20, 1782. Many bald eagles make Alaska their home.

Polar Bear

The polar bear is now listed as a threatened species, because of melting ice in the northern sea and oceans.

Humpback Whale

Humpback whales frequent the seas around Alaska in the spring, summer, and autumn. In the winter, they travel to warmer waters around Mexico or Hawai'i.

Economy

Denali National Park

Denali National Park is one of the most popular tourist destinations in Alaska. It attracts more than 425,000 visitors a year.

Tourism

Tourism is a highly profitable industry in Alaska that has grown in the past several decades. Most visitors come from elsewhere in the United States. Because of Alaska's cold winters and mild summers, most tourists come to the state during summer.

Cruise ships sail along Alaska's coast and bring passengers to the state. Many of the cruises begin in Canada or Seattle, Washington, and sail along the Inside Passage, a waterway between Alaska's southeastern coast and offshore islands. A favorite part of these trips is Glacier Bay, where visitors admire the beautiful ice forms.

Some of the most popular tourist destinations in Alaska are Portage Glacier, Denali National Park, Skagway's historical gold rush district, and the Anchorage Museum of History and Art. The Ketchikan Totems and Sitka's Russian church and dancers also draw large numbers of tourists. Various tours featuring cultural, historical, or wildlife themes are available to help visitors navigate this massive state.

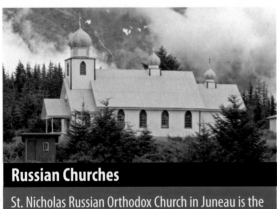

Russian Churches

St. Nicholas Russian Orthodox Church in Juneau is the oldest church in Alaska. It was consecrated in 1894.

Klondike Gold Rush National Historic Park

The city of Skagway is located within the boundaries of Klondike Gold Rush National Historic Park. It is one of only two U.S. cities within a National Park Service site.

Inside Passage

Seeing Alaska from the deck of a cruise ship is a popular vacation trip. Some cruises offer land tours before or after the cruise.

Spanning more than 800 miles, the Trans-Alaska Pipeline crosses more than 800 rivers and streams, as well as three mountain ranges.

Primary Industries

Alaska's first major industry was the fur trade. Russian explorers took furs back to Russia to sell. Though fur trapping still exists in Alaska, it now occurs on a much smaller scale.

The gold industry brought the next big flow of money into the state. Once gold was discovered in the Yukon, scores of prospectors hoping to make it rich moved to Alaska. Like the fur trade, gold mining continues in Alaska but on a much smaller scale.

25 percent of all the **oil** produced by the United States comes from **Alaska**.

Alaska provides most of the **crab**, **salmon**, **halibut**, and **herring** sold in the U.S.

The oil and natural gas industry became important in Alaska in the 1970s. A large oil field was discovered near Prudhoe Bay in 1968. Geologists estimated that it was twice as large as any other oil field in North America at the time. Several oil companies joined together to build the Trans-Alaska Pipeline, which was then the largest privately-funded construction project in history. The pipeline, which cost $8 billion to build, is operated by the Alyeska Pipeline Service Company. It is one of the top tourist attractions in the state.

Today, more Alaskans work in the service sector than in any other part of the economy. Tourism and the government are leading service employers. Timber and fishing are other major industries in the state.

Value of Goods and Services (in Millions of Dollars)

This pie chart shows how important different industries are to Alaska. What is the largest industry in the state? In which categories do you think tourism plays a role?

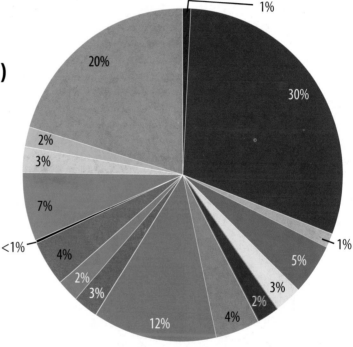

● Agriculture, Forestry, Fishing $1,821	● Media & Entertainment $5,166
● Mining $60,102	● Finance, Insurance & Real Estate $4,296
● Utilities $2,826	● Professional & Technical Services $8,697
● Construction $9,582	● Education $550
● Manufacturing $5,401	● Healthcare $13,301
● Wholesale Trade $4,869	● Hotels & Restaurants $5,449
● Retail Trade $8,688	● Other Services $3,458
● Transportation & Warehousing $24,805	● Government $40,308

Goods and Services

Few goods and services can be found outside the major population centers in Alaska. The best place for people to find what they need is in Anchorage. Most goods found in Anchorage have been flown into the city from elsewhere in the United States. The state's largest airport also is in Anchorage. It is one of the leading handlers of **cargo** in the United States. Some Alaskans are dependent on air travel for the distribution of goods because not all areas have roads or railroads. In fact, Alaska has more registered pilots **per capita** than any other state.

Seaplanes, planes on skis, or small single engine planes are all used to transport goods and people to all areas of Alaska.

Because so many goods and materials have to be brought into the state, Alaska has a high cost of living. The cost of goods is high in Alaska because there is little or no competition. In smaller towns, food may cost up to double what it costs in other places in the United States. Providing services and medical care to remote areas in Alaska is also expensive. The high cost of living has created higher than average salaries. By charging more for their services, Alaskans can offset the high cost of living.

In Alaska's major cities, the cost to feed the average family is $122 per week. In rural areas, the cost is much higher.

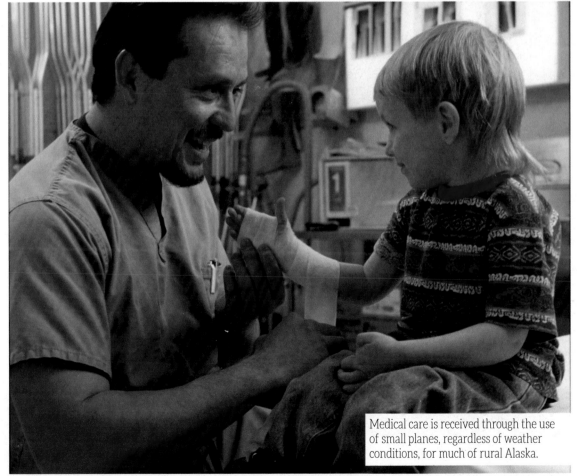

Medical care is received through the use of small planes, regardless of weather conditions, for much of rural Alaska.

The Aleut are native to the Aleutian Islands, and are closely related to the Inuit in language and culture.

Native Americans

Many scientists believe that people have been living in Alaska for 15,000 years or more. The first people to live in North America may have walked from eastern Russia to Alaska over a land bridge that connected the two areas during the last Ice Age, when sea levels were lower than they are today. These people were the **ancestors** of today's Native Americans.

Other native groups may have come to Alaska from eastern Asia by boat or by walking across frozen seas. These groups include the Inuit, or Eskimo, Aleut, and Alutiiq peoples. The Aleut and Alutiiq are from the south and southwest area of Alaska and are culturally and economically tied to the sea.

Each native group that first settled the Alaska region brought with them their own beliefs and creation myths. Most of these beliefs have the sea as a central figure. The stories often explain how the land was created and how the people came to live on it.

Native American groups living in Alaska today include a number of peoples in central and northern Alaska who speak related Athabascan languages. Native American groups in Alaska also include the Northwest Coast peoples of southeastern Alaska, such as the Tlingit, Haida, and Tsimshian peoples.

The cultures of all of Alaska's native peoples are still rich and alive. While many Alaska Natives live modern lives, some still rely on traditional methods of hunting and fishing for food. Many Alaska Natives keep their traditions alive, telling the stories, singing the songs, and dancing the dances that have come down to them from their ancestors.

Today, Native Alaskans continue to celebrate their traditions at events such as the Midnight Sun Intertribal Pow-Wow in Fairbanks, Alaska.

Exploring the Land

In the 1720s, Tsar Peter the Great of Russia sent Vitus Bering to explore the North Pacific Ocean. His goal was to find a northeastern sea route to China around Siberia. Because of bad weather, Bering was unable to see the North American coast on this trip.

In 1741, during the reign of Empress Anna, Bering made a second voyage, and this time he came upon what is now Alaska. Bering died during the return journey. The Russian island on which he is buried is now named Bering Island in his honor. His crew members brought back high-quality sea otter furs from Alaska.

Timeline of Settlement

Russian Settlement

1784 Grigory Shelekhov establishes the first European settlement near present-day Kodiak.

1806 The Russian-American Company, which is allowed by the Russian government to control the fur trade in Alaska, moves its headquarters to Sitka.

1742 Bering crew members bring furs back to Russia.

1824 Russia signs treaties with the United States and Great Britain, establishing trade boundaries and commercial regulations in Alaska.

1741 Vitus Bering, a Dane exploring for Russia, lands near Mount St. Elias.

United States Possession

Early Exploration

1867 After negotiations led by Secretary of State William Seward, the United States purchases Alaska from Russia for $7.2 million.

Bering's successful voyage led to other Russian expeditions, and soon a number of camps had been set up from which Russians trapped sea otters and other fur-bearing animals or traded with the native peoples for furs. In 1784, the first permanent European settlement in what is now Alaska was built on Kodiak Island. From there, Aleksandr Baranov controlled the trapping and trading posts on the mainland. Although Russians controlled Alaska during the late 1700s, explorers from other countries also came to the area, including Captain James Cook and George Vancouver of Great Britain and Juan Perez of Spain.

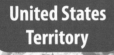

United States Territory

1912 Alaska becomes a U.S. territory

1942 The Japanese invade the Aleutian Islands during World War II.

1942–1945 The Japanese invasion prompts construction of airfields and the Alaska Highway, which contribute to settlement after the war.

1897–1900 The Klondike Gold Rush brings thousands of settlers to Alaska.

Statehood and After

1959 Alaska becomes the 49th state.

1878 Salmon canneries are built in Alaska, starting what was to become the largest salmon industry in the world.

1968 The largest oil field in North America is discovered near Prudhoe Bay.

The First Settlers

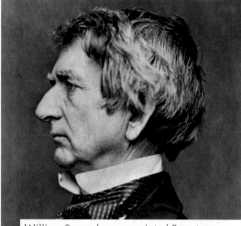

In the mid-1800s, Russia lost interest in Alaska because it was not seeing enough of a profit from the fur trade. Russia offered to sell the land to the United States. U.S. Secretary of State William Seward negotiated a treaty with Russia for the purchase. The treaty, signed in 1867, paid the Russian government $7.2 million for the region. This was less than two cents an acre.

William Seward was appointed Secretary of State by Abraham Lincoln. He managed international affairs during the Civil War.

Newspapers in the United States strongly criticized Seward for the purchase. Many believed Alaska had little to offer the United States. They referred to the deal as "Seward's Folly" and to Alaska as "Seward's Icebox." Despite the objections, the U.S. Senate approved the treaty. Seward's critics quickly forgave him when gold was discovered in the region in the 1870s and 1880s.

The cession of Alaska was signed by the U.S. Secretary of State and the Russian minister to the United States, who was there as a representative for the Emperor of All the Russias.

The discovery of gold encouraged many settlers to come to Alaska in search of fortune. Large gold deposits were found near Nome, Juneau, and Fairbanks. Many of the early settlers were not prepared for Alaska's cold climate. Those who came unprepared faced starvation and exposure to freezing temperatures. Settlers came so quickly that there were few government laws to control the masses. Alaska became known as the Wild North.

Gold discoveries were made in the neighboring Yukon Territory as well. Traffic through Alaska increased as prospectors made their way to Canada. Settlements grew into communities with churches, newspapers, and other services. In 1906, Juneau replaced Sitka as Alaska's capital. In the same year Alaska adopted a code of laws and a court system.

The Yukon Trail was the shortest and least expensive travel option at the time of the Klondike Gold Rush.

During the Klondike Gold Rush, many prospectors lost their lives due to the harsh climate and poor living conditions.

History Makers

Many notable Alaskans have contributed to the development of their state and their country. These include Alaska Natives who helped win equality for their people. They also include a man who helped to make Alaska a state and a teenager who created the Alaskan flag. In addition, several writers have communicated the beauty and wonder of Alaska to the world as a whole.

Leonhard Seppala (1877-1967)

Leonhard Seppala is one of the greatest sled dog racers Alaska has ever known. He was born in Norway and came to Alaska as a young man, attracted by the Gold Rush. In 1914, he began to win sled dog races and became a legend in his own time. He is most known for rushing diphtheria medicine to Nome, Alaska, in 1925, when the city faced a deadly outbreak of the disease.

Ernest Gruening (1887–1974)

When Alaska was still a territory, Ernest Gruening served as both the governor and a senator, although he could not yet vote in the Senate. He led the drive for Alaska's statehood and then served as senator from Alaska from 1959 to 1969.

Carl Ben Eielson (1897–1929)

Carl Ben Eielson trained as a pilot during World War I. In 1925, he was the first person to fly over the polar ice cap, from Alaska to Greenland. Eielson died in a plane crash in 1929, while trying to rescue passengers aboard a ship caught in the ice off the Siberian coast.

Elizabeth Peratrovich (1911–1958)

A Tlingit Native American, Elizabeth Peratrovich was no stranger to discrimination in Alaska. In 1945, Peratrovich provided testimony to the Alaska Senate that led to the passage of an antidiscrimination law. This law required equal treatment for all citizens in public accommodations.

John Ben "Benny" Benson (1913–1972)

In 1927, 13-year-old Benny Benson's design for a flag for Alaska was chosen in a contest. When Alaska became a state, the drafters of the Alaska constitution required that Benson's design become the official flag of the state of Alaska. Benson worked as a carpenter and mechanic for Kodiak Airways until his death in 1972.

Once called Eskimos, the Inuit are ethnically very different than the Native Americans in the lower 48 states. There are between 25,000 to 35,000 Inuit in Alaska today.

Anchorage is located at the head of Cook Inlet and is a year-round seaport for international shipping. Today, the current economy relies on oil production.

The People Today

Although Alaska's population is small, it has steadily increased over the past several decades. In 1980, Alaska's population was just over 400,000. By 2000, the state had more than 625,000 residents, an increase of more than 50 percent in those 20 years. By 2012, the state had more than 730,000 residents. About 300,000 people live in the state's largest city, Anchorage. Fairbanks and Juneau are both home to over 32,000 people respectively. Wasilla is the only other city in the state to have more than 10,000 residents, and numerous cities have fewer than 150 residents.

Many of today's Alaskans are descendants of early Russian settlers or of Americans and Canadians who came in search of gold in the late 1800s. Native peoples account for about 15 percent of Alaska's population. Although some Alaska Natives live in cities, most live in smaller towns and villages. The state's population also includes small numbers of Hispanics, African Americans, and Asian Americans. Most of these people live in cities.

Alaska's population **increased** by **more than 100,000** people since **2000**.

Q What are some of the reasons that Alaska's relatively small population has grown in recent years?

State Government

Like each state in the Union, Alaska is governed on local, state, and federal levels. The state has a governor and a lieutenant governor, both of whom are elected to four-year terms. The governor appoints the head of each of the 14 state departments.

William A. Egan served as Alaska's first governor, and Bob Bartlett as the state's first senator, after Alaska's admission to the Union.

The state legislature has two chambers, the Senate and the House of Representatives. Forty representatives are elected to the House every two years. Twenty senators are elected every four years. Local government is not divided into counties as in other states. Instead, the state is divided into cities and **boroughs**.

Sarah Palin, the former governor of Alaska, ran as the vice presidential candidate under John McCain in the 2008 presidential race.

On January 3, 1959, Alaska became the 49th state to join the Union. The only state admitted to the Union after Alaska was Hawai'i. Alaska is represented in Washington, D.C., by two members of the U.S. Senate and one member of the U.S. House of Representatives.

In 1971, the U.S. Congress approved the Claims Settlement Act. This act granted 44 million acres of land and more than $950 million to Alaska's native peoples. This unprecedented act legitimized the ownership of land the Native Alaskans had always considered culturally their own.

Alaska's state song is called
"Alaska."

*Eight stars of gold on a field of blue,
Alaska's flag, may it mean to you,
The blue of the sea, the evening sky,
The mountain lakes and
the flowers nearby,*

*The gold of the early sourdough's dreams,
The precious gold of the hills and streams,
The brilliant stars in the northern sky,
The "Bear," the "Dipper," and shining high,*

*The great North Star with its steady light,
O'er land and sea a beacon light,
Alaska's flag to Alaskans dear,
The simple flag of a last frontier.*

* excerpted

President Jimmy Carter signed the Alaska National Interest Lands Conservation Act into federal law in 1980. This law advocates the conservation of more than 157 million acres of land in Alaska.

The Klukwan, one of Alaska's native groups, celebrate the bald eagle during the annual Eagle Festival.

Celebrating Culture

Alaska Natives make up the largest minority group in Alaska. Long before Russians or other explorers first traveled to the region, native peoples such as Inuit, Aleuts, and Native American groups had their own rich cultures. They had their own belief systems, ceremonies, and arts and crafts. They used the resources available to them for practical and ceremonial purposes. For example, they carved ivory from walrus tusks to make harpoon heads and knife handles. They also carved dolls and sculptures from ivory. Jade and soapstone were also used in carvings. Many of the ancient arts and crafts traditions of Alaska Natives continue today.

Tingit people often use masks in cultural ceremonies. Different masks represented different spirit guides.

The Northwest Coast Native Americans who live in the southeastern part of the state continue to build totem poles. Totem poles are carved from huge cedar trees. They record the history, culture, and life events of the people who carve them. Totem poles include symbols for ancestors or **clans**. They are painted with vegetable or mineral dyes.

Often, when people think of living in Alaska, igloos come to mind. Very few people use igloos anymore. However, igloos are still used by Inuit hunters out on the frozen ocean or tundra. They are built as temporary shelters for the period of the hunt.

Ketchikan, Alaska features more than 80 totem poles. Visitors can experience several of them during a walking tour of the area.

Historically, canoes were the Native Alaskan's main transport system for a variety of tasks. Today Native Alaskans use them as a way of connecting to their past.

Visitors to Alaska can take advantage of several northern lights tours. Peak viewing is when the weather is coldest and darkest, at the end of December and into January.

Arts and Entertainment

Although the northern lights are not an art form, they could be. Also called the aurora borealis, these dancing lights provide one of the best forms of entertainment in the state. Northern lights are naturally occurring colored lights in the upper atmosphere. They are most visible near Earth's magnetic poles. Fairbanks is considered one of the best places in the world to see the northern lights.

Anchorage is an excellent place to be immersed in Alaskan culture. The city boasts art galleries, museums, theaters, a symphony orchestra, and an opera house. The Anchorage Museum of History and Art houses a gallery showing works of art from Alaska and around the world. The museum also displays artifacts from several Alaskan cultures.

In 1946, the **Anchorage Symphony Orchestra** became the first of three symphonies in Alaska.

Since 2005, Alaska has become a **reality star**. In 2014, there were more than **20 reality shows** being filmed in the state to highlight its **unique culture**.

The Heritage Library and Museum in Anchorage features artwork by Alaska Natives and other Alaskans, including tools, paintings, costumes, and beadwork. Fairbanks has rich historical architecture, and Juneau boasts the Juneau-Douglas City Museum, featuring the Tlingit culture and exhibits on the early gold-mining experience.

Alaska hosts numerous festivals, fairs, and celebrations throughout the year. Many festivals occur during the summer months, when the sun shines almost around the clock. Most towns have activities to celebrate the **summer solstice**.

A singer-songwriter, guitarist, and poet, Jewel grew up on an 800-acre homestead in Homer, Alaska, with no running water or electricity.

The Alaska State Fair is held about an hour north of Anchorage. The fair strives to showcase the state's unique beauty.

Dog sledding was necessary to the success of the fur trade in Alaska. Modern dog sledding is mostly for recreation.

Sports and Recreation

One of the most popular sports in Alaska is dog mushing, or sled dog racing. In fact, it was adopted as Alaska's official state sport in 1972. Hundreds of races ranging from local matches to world championships are held every year. There are different kinds of races, from sprint mushing to long-distance racing. Winners of sprint races are determined by speed, often over distances of 12 to 15 miles. Long-distance races can take many days, even weeks, as the racers travel great distances.

The Iditarod Trail Sled Dog Race is one of the oldest races run in Alaska. First held as a 56-mile race in 1967, the Iditarod was made into a much longer 1,100-mile race in 1973. The race starts in Anchorage and goes up and across the state, ending in Nome. Today, winners often take about nine days to finish the course.

In 1985, **Libby Riddles** became the **first woman** to win the **Iditarod**.

Seward's **Chad Bentz** made history as the second Major League Baseball player to field and catch after being born with **only one hand**.

For four days in July, native peoples from Alaska, the Pacific Northwest, and Canada gather in Fairbanks for the World Eskimo-Indian Olympics. Traditional Alaskan competitions are held, including ear-pulling, a four-man carry, knuckle hopping, and **high kicking**.

The World Eskimo-Indian Olympics begin with a race called the Race of the Torch. The race winner lights the Olympic torch that year.

The Great Alaska Shootout is a college basketball tournament in Anchorage that takes place over Thanksgiving. The tournament attracts some of the best NCAA teams from around the country. Aside from basketball, other popular sports in Alaska include skiing, kayaking, and baseball.

The first World Eskimo-Indian Olympics was held in Fairbanks in 1961. The games work to preserve the cultural heritage of Native Alaskans.

Get To Know
ALASKA

There are more than **70** active **volcanoes** in Alaska.

Alaska has the lowest population density of any other state in the U.S., with 1 person per square mile.

The world's largest rechargeable battery, weighing **1,400 tons** is located in Fairbanks, Alaska.

ALASKA'S COASTLINE IS MORE THAN 6,600 MILES LONG.

Waking a sleeping bear for the purpose of taking a photo is **illegal** in Alaska.

Alaska is known for giant vegetables, like the 94-pound cabbage once grown there.

With more than **1 million** seals, the Pribilof Islands are home to the **largest seal colony** in the **world**.

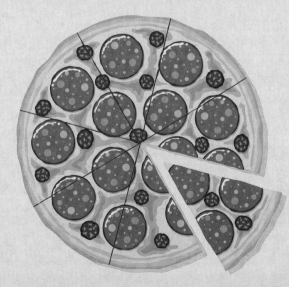

Pizza lovers can have a **pizza** delivered by **plane** in Alaska.

Brain Teasers

What have you learned about Alaska after reading this book? Test your knowledge by answering these questions. All of the information can be found in the text you just read. The answers are provided below for easy reference.

1 What is the state mammal of Alaska?

2 Which city is the largest by area?

3 What are Alaska's two main foreign exports?

4 Which Native Alaskan group is known for making totem poles?

5 In what year did Alaska become the 49th state?

6 Who designed Alaska's state flag?

7 How many members make up Alaska's House of Representatives?

8 What is the name of the 1,100-mile dogsled race that starts in Anchorage and ends in Nome?

Key Words

ancestors: ancient relatives

boroughs: units of local government similar to counties in other states

cargo: goods transported by ships, trucks, and airplanes

clans: groups of families

ecosystems: a community of living things

exports: shipments to other countries

glaciers: large, slow-moving sheets of ice

high kicking: an Inuit sporting activity in which competitors jump up and kick a hanging object

per capita: in relation to the size of a population

prospectors: individuals who search for gold

spawn: to give birth

summer solstice: the beginning of summer in the Northern Hemisphere

threatened: referring to a type of plant or animal that is likely to become endangered, or at risk of disappearing from Earth

tundra: large, treeless plains in the Arctic with a top layer that remains frozen throughout the year

Index

Alaska Natives 7, 17, 27, 32, 35, 38, 41
Anchorage 21, 24, 35, 40, 41, 42, 43, 46

bald eagles 19, 38
Benson, John Ben "Benny" 33
Bering, Vitus 28, 29

Canada 21, 31, 43
climate 3, 7, 12, 31
crafts 38

Denali 5, 8, 9, 11, 20, 21
dog mushing 32, 42

Eielson, Carl Ben 33
exports 14, 46

Fairbanks 27, 31, 35, 40, 41, 43
fur trade 7, 22, 28, 30, 42

glaciers 5, 9, 10, 21
gold 7, 14, 15, 21, 22, 29, 30, 31, 32, 35, 37, 41
Gruening, Ernest 33

Iditarod 42, 46
igloos 39

Juneau 4, 8, 9, 21, 31, 35, 41, 46

mining 7, 14, 15, 22, 23, 41
museums 21, 40, 41

Nome 31, 32, 42, 46
northern lights 5, 9, 40

oil 15, 22, 23, 29, 35, 44

Palin, Sarah 36
Peratrovich, Elizabeth 33
plants 9, 11, 16

Russia 7, 22, 27, 28, 30

salmon 14, 18, 22, 29
Seppala, Leonhard 32
Seward, William 28, 30
Sitka 21, 28, 31
Skagway 21

temperature 12, 17, 31
totem poles 39, 46
Trans-Alaska Pipeline 15, 22, 23
tundra 5, 39, 47

World Eskimo-Indian Olympics 43

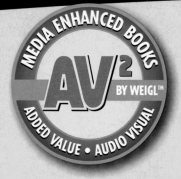

Log on to www.av2books.com

AV[2] by Weigl brings you media enhanced books that support active learning. Go to www.av2books.com, and enter the special code found on page 2 of this book. You will gain access to enriched and enhanced content that supplements and complements this book. Content includes video, audio, weblinks, quizzes, a slide show, and activities.

AV[2] Online Navigation

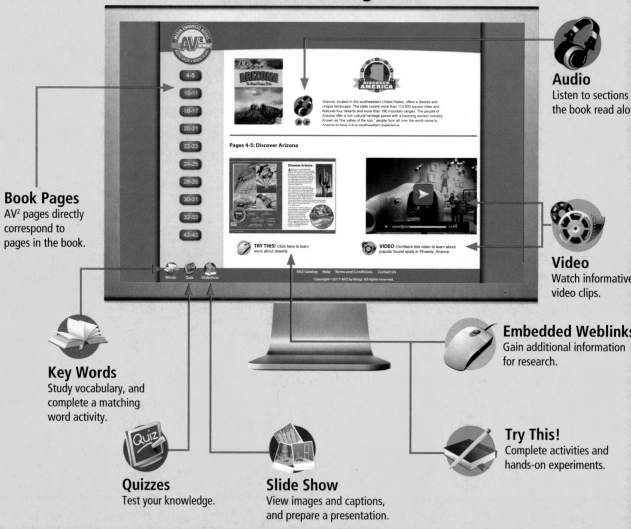

Book Pages
AV[2] pages directly correspond to pages in the book.

Audio
Listen to sections
the book read alou

Video
Watch informative
video clips.

Key Words
Study vocabulary, and complete a matching word activity.

Embedded Weblinks
Gain additional information for research.

Quizzes
Test your knowledge.

Slide Show
View images and captions, and prepare a presentation.

Try This!
Complete activities and hands-on experiments.

AV[2] was built to bridge the gap between print and digital. We encourage you to tell us what you like and what you want to see in the future.

Sign up to be an AV[2] Ambassador at www.av2books.com/ambassador.